MW00412243

AWAKENING
THE GIANTS

SHANE W ROESSIGER

Copyright © 2018 SHANE W ROESSIGER

All rights reserved.

ISBN-13: 978-1720776932
ISBN-10: 1720776938

DEDICATION

" To each member of this glorious Body, called Christ..."

CONTENTS

Precious Saints in Christ,

First of all, we want to thank our Lord Jesus Christ for choosing us as earthly vessels. It is an honor to be used by Him in any way, and we will serve Him and you, His children, with the fear of the Lord.

Today, what we are bringing to you is not just information but revelation and impartation of spiritual gifts so that you may grow into the knowledge of Him and walk into your destiny.

H.O.T. HOUSE OF TRUTH is a division of In Him Healing Touch Ministry. We are a small but powerful part of the Body of Christ that is totally surrendered to Jesus Christ and His kingdom. **We chose to be HOT for Him (Revelation 3:15-17).** We love the church of Jesus Christ, and we decided to give ourselves up for her until we see every member of the Body of Jesus growing into the fullness of Him. We operate in all the gifts of the Spirit. We desire the fruits of the Spirit inside of us, and we will not stop until we see His glory covering the World. Our team flows together in the prophetic, and we all submit one to another as the Holy Spirit leads. It's not about one man but about **THE MAN, JESUS CHRIST.**

Every one of our H.O.T. team prays that you will be even more on fire for HIM than ever before and will use every single spiritual gift and every bit of compassion to reach the lost and to spread the true love of Jesus to all mankind.

You get ready: God is more than willing to do a new thing today! Some of you have been drinking from the old wine and have said, "This wine is good enough," but it is not **(Luke 5: 35-50)**. There is a huge banquet set before all of us. He is about to transform water into new wine **(John 2: 1-11)**. It is time for the Body of Christ to stop rejecting what God is bringing to the table: the new wine!

We are very excited to be here because God is giving us a message to the Body of Christ and to the leaders: It is time to bring an apostolic alignment to the church of Jesus Christ, to raise up men and women to become disciples, to pull out gifts that have been buried through religion and control, and to break mindsets of the church so that the Body of Christ can walk having Jesus as the head!

We prophesy **Ephesians 1:17-23** over you, member of the precious Body of Christ.

"That the God of our Lord Jesus Christ, the Father of glory, may give unto you the **spirit of wisdom and revelation in the knowledge of him**: **The eyes of your understanding being enlightened**; that ye may know what is **the hope of his calling**, and what is the **riches of the glory of his inheritance in the saints**, And what is the exceeding greatness of **his power to us-ward who believe**, according to the **working of his mighty power**, Which he wrought in Christ, when he raised him from the dead, and set him at his own right hand in the heavenly places, **Far above all principality, and power, and might, and**

dominion, and every name that is named, not only in this world, but also in that which is to come: And hath put all things under his feet, and **gave him to be the head over all things to the church**, Which is **his body**, the fullness of him that filleth all in all.

Amen! In Him, we love you,

Your servant,

Shane W Roessiger

www.hothouseoftruth.com

SHANE W ROESSIGER

.

1
TAKING THE FIRST STEP

"Remember not the former things, neither consider the things
of old. Behold, I will do a new thing, now it shall spring forth;
shall you not know it?..."
Isaiah 43: 18-19

It is time to empty ourselves of all old religious thinking
and traditions. This latter rain shall be greater than the former
(Zechariah 10:1). This is not about what we like or what we
want. Be open to having your mind totally transformed. God
refuses to work in the old system any longer. God is changing
everything, but in reality, He is bringing things back to the
way the disciples operated in the beginning but with
exceedingly more glory! He is saving the best for last! He will
not put new wine into old bottles, into old traditions, into old

ways of doing things **(Matthew 9:14-17)**.

Are you ready to let the old go and embrace the new?

The Lord will not mix the old and the new. He will rip off everything that is old FIRST, so He can come with the new. He will start with the foundation of the modern day church. He is breaking down man-made foundations, and He is restoring the cornerstone and rebuilding again on the apostles and the prophets. This is why we are going back to the first church, how the church started. God is saying to the Body of Christ, "Build, build, build on the rock!"

Churches built on the sand: Man-made foundations.

Churches built on the rock: Apostolic churches.

Ephesians 2:19-22

UPON THIS ROCK I WILL BUILD MY CHURCH

We are in the building process and the foundation is set. The foundation is **JESUS CHRIST,** *the* **rock (Matthew 7:24-27)**. We are calling out wise men to build a house that will stand. We are going to build on the power of the cross and the blood that sets us free. His Word is Truth. This is **HIS HOUSE,** and we are HIS hands. **HIS blueprint** is being manifested in this region. It is not about any denomination. We are not building upon any man's foundation **(Romans 15:20)** but on the rock **(Luke 6:46-49)**. This house built on the rock will stand the test of time. His glory will fill this place. His truth will go around the World from here. **Some say, "No," but we say, "Yes!" Are you ready?**

2
DIVINE APOSTOLIC ALIGNMENT

It is time for an apostolic alignment. Let's bring back the divine order to the Body of Christ.

Church, arise and shine! Order is coming back to the body. Not the order that religion tries to put on you. This reformation is a divine order. Not a man-made hierarchy, but a body full of ALL MEMBERS and parts that are back in order. Break down the man-made foundation. GOD has placed gifts in everyone, from the head to the whole Body of Christ (**1 Corinthians 3:4**).

"**And he gave some to be apostles; and some prophets; and some evangelists; and some pastors and teachers.**" **Ephesians 4:11**

For what? "For the perfecting of the saints, for the work of the ministry, for the edifying of the body of Christ:" Ephesians 4: 12

Which purpose? "Till we all come in the unity of the faith, and of the knowledge of the Son of God, unto a perfect man, unto the measure of the stature of the fullness of Christ: That we henceforth be no more children, tossed to and fro, and carried about with every wind of doctrine, by the sleight of men, and cunning craftiness, whereby they lie in wait to deceive; But speaking the truth in love, may grow up into him in all things, which is the head, even Christ: From whom the whole body fitly joined together and compacted by that which every joint supplieth, according to the effectual working in the measure of every part, maketh increase of the body unto the edifying of itself in love." Ephesians 4: 13-16

"Now therefore ye are no more strangers and foreigners, but fellow citizens with the saints, and of the household of God; And are built upon the foundation of the apostles and prophets, Jesus Christ himself being the chief cornerstone; In whom all the building fitly framed together groweth unto an holy temple in the Lord: In whom ye also are builded together for an habitation of God through the Spirit." Ephesians 2:19-22

"For every house is built by someone, but HE who built all things is God." Hebrews 3: 4

God is taking back THE CHIEF CORNERSTONE to the foundation of His church. **"The cornerstone which the builder refused is become the head stone of the corner."** Psalms 118: 22

AWAKENING THE FIVE GIANTS IN THE LAND

Who are the FIVE GIANTS IN THE LAND?
THE FIVEFOLD MINISTRIES
According to **Ephesians Chapter 4**

"Church, line up!" God says, "Now is the time for apostolic alignment." God has given all different gifts, mantles, and anointing for the work of the ministry and the equipping of the saints. When leaders hide the gifts in the back room, they are saying, "Hey, Jesus, we don't want you to operate here. We want you to just sit down and listen." This is exactly how God sees it when we don't allow full operation of the Spirit. Man's order must be shut down and full alliance must take place for regions to be shaken on behalf of the lost. They are the pearl of great price that need to be found!

We need the whole body working together. Not just one man, the PASTOR, but we need the entire Body of Christ working together! It's time to wake up and take the land!

Because of the lack of knowledge and revelation in the church today, we have elevated this position, PASTOR, to be *the* high calling. However, the truth is that in God's order none of the gifts are better or higher than the other. They all

7

must work together to reveal Jesus or else the body looks like a freak. The Bible says in **Ephesians 4: 16: "From whom the whole body fitly joined together compacted by that which every joint supplies according to the effectual working in the measure of every part, making increase of the body to every part, unto the edifying of itself."**

THE BODY OF CHRIST:
EVERY MEMBER WORKING TOGETHER

"For the body is not one member, but many." 1 Corinthians 12:14

What about me? I'm just a toe of the Body? There is room for every member of the Body of Christ.

"If the foot should say, "Because I am not a hand, I am not of the body," is it therefore not of the body? [16] And if the ear should say, "Because I am not an eye, I am not of the body," is it therefore not of the body? If the whole body *were* an eye, where *would be* the hearing? If the whole *were* hearing, where *would be* the smelling? But now God has set the members, each one of them, in the body just as He pleased. And if they were all one member, where *would* the body *be?* But now indeed *there are* many members, yet one body. And the eye cannot say to the hand, "I have no need of

you"; nor again the head to the feet, "I have no need of you." No, much rather, those members of the body which seem to be weaker are necessary."1 Corinthians 12:15-22

First of all, let's make this clear: the temple is NOT the building. **YOU ARE THE TEMPLE.**

"Know ye not that ye are the temple of God, and that the Spirit
of God dwelleth in you?" 1 Corinthians 3: 16

Members of the Body of Christ, you are mighty!

"And God has appointed these in the church: first apostles, second prophets, third teachers, after that miracles, then gifts of healings, helps, administrations, varieties of tongues. *Are* all apostles? *Are* all prophets? *Are* all teachers? *Are* all workers of miracles? Do all have gifts of healings? Do all speak with tongues? Do all interpret? But earnestly desire the best gifts. And yet I show you a more excellent way." 1 Corinthians 12: 28-31

We see the Body of Christ fully moving and working together, joined together as ONE! It's all about the Kingdom. God wants us all to be a part of His kingdom. Let's look at the ants and learn from their example. They work in unity in all they know and do. You don't ever see one colony operating differently from one another.

"Now we are the Body of Christ, and members in particular. And God has set some in the church, first apostles, secondarily prophets, thirdly teachers after that miracles, the gifts of healing, helps, governments, diversities of tongues." 1 Corinthians 12:28

We are the temple of God!

A church is not made by the hands of men, nor is the church a building. A church is a gathering of saints, a gathering of the members of the **BODY OF CHRIST**. God has anointed His members and has placed gifts inside each of us. Sadly, gifts are just sitting and being wasted; that is, until now. The gifts are there to build up the Body so the Body can grow strong and take the land.

Paul is clearly saying in **Ephesians 4: 2-7** that we are to do this with lowliness and meekness, with longsuffering, forbearing with one another in love: one body and one Spirit - one faith and one God! So, we all need to move in God, in one accord, not one member or gift preferred above the other. A high calling should be whatever God has called YOU to do: "Come on, Church. Now let's go and take our places!"

"For our comely parts have no need; but God has tempered the

Body together, having given move abundant honor to the part which lacked that there should be no schisms in the Body that the members should have the same care one for another." 1 Corinthians 12:24-25

We are all members of one body: THE BODY OF CHRIST! We need to submit one to another. The head needs to submit to the toe and the toe to the head!

DIFFERENCE BETWEEN SUBMISSION AND CONTROL

Today the word submission has a bad connotation, but this is because of the lack of understanding. Everything started in the garden, when Eve did not understand the powerful beauty of submission. Let's not make the same mistake. Let's now get some understanding and revelation about it.

"Giving thanks always for all things unto God and the Father in the name of our Lord Jesus Christ;

Submitting yourselves one to another in the fear of God.

Wives, submit yourselves unto your own husbands, as unto the Lord. For the husband is the head of the wife, even as Christ is the head of the church: and he is the saviour of the body.

Therefore as the church is subject unto Christ, so let the wives be to their own husbands in everything.

Husbands, love your wives, even as Christ also loved the church, and gave himself for it;

That he might sanctify and cleanse it with the washing of water by the word,

That he might present it to himself a glorious church, not having spot, or wrinkle, or any such thing; but that it should be holy and without blemish.

So ought men to love their wives as their own bodies. He that loveth his wife loveth himself.

For no man ever yet hated his own flesh; but nourisheth and cherisheth it, even as the Lord the church:

For we are members of his body, of his flesh, and of his bones.

For this cause shall a man leave his father and mother, and shall be joined unto his wife, and they two shall be one flesh.

This is a great mystery: but I speak concerning Christ and the church.

Nevertheless let every one of you in particular so love his wife even as himself; and the wife see that she reverence her husband." Ephesians 5:20-33

First of all, let's think why the church is acting like the world? It's a Jezebel spirit. The church has opened doors of pleasing people! Satan is seducing people with their idols and using flattery and false fruits.

"I know thy works, and charity, and service, and faith, and thy patience, and thy works; and the last to be more than the first.

Notwithstanding I have a few things against thee, because thou sufferest that woman Jezebel, which calleth herself a prophetess, to teach and to seduce my servants to commit fornication, and to eat things sacrificed unto idols.

And I gave her space to repent of her fornication; and she repented not." Revelation 2:19-21

When you do not obey the Word of God, you make yourself an open target for deception. God has divine order. Even the world knows about order. They stole it from God. Order keeps the peace; order protects people. Yes, when you have bad and corrupt leaders or authority, you begin to be controlled and dictated, but this still does not make God a liar or give you a right to dismantle His ways. Satan makes God words into bad words! The world does the same. It's called anti-Christ. It's a spirit of perversion. It perverts the right ways, twisting order and twisting scripture to make it what they want.

That is why you see lesbian married woman now in leadership in some so-called churches. They call themselves apostles, but they are not. The women's movement and equal rights were really not good for women. There is a war against God, not women. We have the same movement in the church, with Jezebel and independent spirits. What happened every year in this country since this movement? We have become more perverted and immoral on a drastic scale because it was breaking God's laws and making submission a bad word. Now we have false freedom, maverick movements. Women carry the same mindset in the church; so do men! They say I only submit to Jesus. That's good, but you really don't. Why, because His Word tells us to submit to the gift in the body and to one another! So, the same perversion creeps in the church, and most churches are run by the Jezebel spirit, and so many only submit to people that think and talk like them. It's called rebellion. The world saw a false love, rebellion movement in the 60's that caused false peace and false love. It's in the church, and it's called apostasy now. The only authentic peace comes from submitting to Jesus and the Truth. False freedom is you do whatever you want; you become your own God. It's the anti-Christ spirit. Real freedom is submitting to God and receiving His true love and peace. This is a false grace, hyper grace movement, but judgment starts in the house of God.

Just because there are religious tyrants does not make us have the right to protest against God and His Word for faulty liars and false leaders. Where there is counterfeit, there is real. God is alive; so is His Body. Rebellious Jezebels will usurp authority. Then they show corrupted reasons why to follow their pernicious ways. They say, "We are free," meanwhile being deceived while they put fear on you that God and man want to control you. This is what they did to destroy marriages in the world. Males and females are coming under the power of Jezebel to seduce you to eat her fornicated teaching and cherry picking doctrine to allure you to her table, then cutting off the head and protection of God in submitting to God and His government, taking our trust in God away. What Satan had to do first was to make the word submission a bad word. Remember, we were all in the world before we were in Christ, under Jezebel's teaching with no anointing. So, if the mind does not get renewed, it will continue to think like the world. In that, you are bringing in your rebellious behaviors because of wounds and hurts, and you have been controlled by them and have made vows against men and leaders. For example, you say, "I will never listen to a man," or "I will never let a man tell me what to do."

Let's see the difference between controlled and submission. One is bad; one is good; but Satan made them both bad and both to mean the same thing. He is a pervert from the beginning.

Submission: The action or fact of accepting or yielding to a superior force or to the will or authority of another person.

So we submit to God and yield to His Word, and then we are protected and shielded.

Controlled, controlling: To exercise restraint or direction over; dominate; command.

If Satan can make God's children make submission look like control, he has you rebelling against God and His government. This brings anarchy and division.

The funny thing is that this is what he did in marriages, wanting to be equal, and we are, but we are not (equal because we are made in His image, and we are loved the same and are his children, but different in the roles that we play and live). God has order. Look at what happens when Satan perverts order. Jezebel makes Ahab out of the man, actually controlling man with seduction and enticements, and makes herself the head and wants you to submit to false freedom. This is what she wants to do to the head, Jesus. We are the bride of Christ, but Jezebel wants to make leaders like Ahab to be man-pleasing and to control and pervert the ways of God, saying we are all equal. It's true, but it's not.

Just like Satan twisted (perverted) Eve in the Garden saying that you're missing out, that God is keeping you from something. You can be like God, and you will not surely die. Satan was perverting the ways of God from the beginning. We, as the body of Christ, were formed and made to fit into our position. When we want to change ourselves into what we want, we pervert the right ways of God and then come out of His protection. If the husband gets out of God's order, meaning becoming Jezebel in the church, there is no hope. Then the wife has to make sure that she is submitting to the Holy Spirit, almost double honor, but if the husband is not in church, the woman can be under God's protection!

"Now the serpent was more subtle than any beast of the field which the LORD God had made. And he said unto the woman, Yea, hath God said, Ye shall not eat of every tree of the garden?
And the woman said unto the serpent, We may eat of the fruit of the trees of the garden: But of the fruit of the tree which is in the midst of the garden, God hath said, Ye shall not eat of it, neither shall ye touch it, lest ye die. And the serpent said unto the woman, Ye shall not surely die: For God doth know

that in the day ye eat thereof, then your eyes shall be opened, and ye shall be as gods, knowing good and evil. And when the woman saw that the tree was good for food, and that it was pleasant to the eyes, and a tree to be desired to make one wise, she took of the fruit thereof, and did eat, and gave also unto her husband with her; and he did eat." Genesis 3:1-6

Read in 1 Corinthians 12: 14-25: "For the body is not one member, but many. If the foot shall say, Because I am not the hand, I am not of the body; is it therefore not of the body? And if the ear shall say, Because I am not the eye, I am not of the body; is it therefore not of the body? If the whole body were an eye, where were the hearing? If the whole were hearing, where were the smelling? But now hath God set the members every one of them in the body, as it hath pleased him. And if they were all one member, where were the body? But now are they many members, yet but one body. And the eye cannot say unto the hand, I have no need of thee: nor again the head to the feet, I have no need of you. Nay, much more those members of the body, which seem to be more feeble, are necessary: And those members of the body, which we think to be less honorable, upon these we bestow more abundant honor; and our uncomely parts have more abundant comeliness. For our comely parts have no need: but God hath tempered the body together, having given more abundant honor to that part which lacked. That there should be no schism in the body; but that the members should have the same care one for another."

It's the same for the body of Christ. When you misplace

yourself or usurp authority, you actually become a pervert. In church, in the world, and in a marriage, whether you sleep with a man, or are a man with a man, or a woman with a woman, in action and mind you are fornicating with rebellion and end up sleeping with Satan. Then you eat from Jezebel's table, not the table of the Lord in sincerity and in truth, turning truth into lies and lies into truth, good words into bad words, and God's ways into your ways.

In the Kingdom of God, there is no male or female in the Spirit.

So, this spirit (Jezebel) can be also for men and women in the church. Let's make submission the good word, order and protection, and God's covering, instead of what Satan has deceived and made into control and domination. He is a liar from the beginning! Live under an open heaven where truth, revelation, and blessing flow.

"Salute all them that have the rule over you, and all the saints. They of Italy salute you. Grace be with you all. Amen." Hebrews 13:24-25

3
ROAD MAP TO FREEDOM

The road map to freedom is this: submission to God (Holy Spirit); submission to His ways; submission to THE Word of God; submission to Christ in one another, the Kingdom of God within.

"Now concerning spiritual gifts, brethren, I would not have you ignorant.

Ye know that ye were Gentiles, carried away unto these dumb idols, even as ye were led. Wherefore I give you to understand, that no man speaking by the Spirit of God calleth Jesus accursed: and that no man can say that Jesus is the Lord, but by the Holy Ghost.

Now there are diversities of gifts, but the same Spirit.

And there are differences of administrations, but the same Lord.

And there are diversities of operations, but it is the same God which worketh all in all.

But the manifestation of the Spirit is given to every man to profit withal.

For to one is given by the Spirit the word of wisdom; to another the word of knowledge by the same Spirit;

To another faith by the same Spirit; to another the gifts of healing by the same Spirit;

To another the working of miracles; to another prophecy; to another discerning of spirits; to another divers kinds of tongues; to another the interpretation of tongues:

But all these worketh that one and the selfsame Spirit, dividing to every man severally as he will.

For as the body is one, and hath many members, and all the members of that one body, being many, are one body: so also is Christ.

For by one Spirit are we all baptized into one body, whether we be Jews or Gentiles, whether we be bond or free; and have been all made to drink into one Spirit." 1 Corinthians 12:1-13

He said, "My children are bound and they are attacked because they love religiosity, they are rebellious, deceived, lacking knowledge, prideful." Minds are being conformed to false grace and man's order, to unbiblical structures that come from Constantine and Protestant and Catholic traditions.

There is a way that seems right but ends in destruction. His ways are always best! "My children, My ways are not your ways." The fear of the Lord is the beginning of wisdom! Satan brings confusion by mixing in leaven in unleavened bread.

We will perish for lack knowledge and understanding. We must understand God's kingdom to benefit from it in our daily lives! Satan is a disrupter, a liar and a thief! He wants to rob our destiny and purpose! He works through children of pride and rebellion! Let God open our eyes as He explains about ascension giftings and gifts of the Holy Spirit! There is a government of God. It is for protection and edification, not lording and controlling His people. That will also be exposed.

ITINERARY ministry is not in the Bible. It came from the Babylonian 5013c beast system. It separates us from Body ministry. This ministry is gifted people running around with a few gifts to make a living from the Gospel. It is prostitution and unbalanced.

The SENT ONES are apostles and prophets. This is what has poisoned the church. No correction, no Truth, just cotton candy words, making people follow their spiritual addiction, making others to become addicted to soothsaying and ear tickling.

God has a government order! It is not about controlling people, but order!

"And he gave some, apostles; and some, prophets; and some, evangelists; and some, pastors and teachers;

For the perfecting of the saints, for the work of the ministry, for the edifying of the body of Christ:

Till we all come in the unity of the faith, and of the knowledge of the Son of God, unto a perfect man, unto the measure of the stature of the fulness of Christ:

That we henceforth be no more children, tossed to and fro, and carried about with every wind of doctrine, by the sleight of men, and cunning craftiness, whereby they lie in wait to deceive;" Ephesians 4:11-14

Satan has been giving out titles like bubble gum. False prophets of Baal have told people in the Body that they are this and that, but they have been sent by the liar, Satan. God tells us first. Then He waits to see who obeys. He will remind us through the Body gifts who are who. There are specific gifts given by God with a specific reason. Even though we are all part of the ministry of reconciliation, there are some people and some offices in the Body ordained with a purpose. God administrates them, not man! The same God that works all in all to profit all! That is why we need to be submitted to one another. Because the true treasure in the Body is Christ in us!

"I therefore, the prisoner of the Lord, beseech you that ye walk worthy of the vocation wherewith ye are called,

With all lowliness and meekness, with longsuffering, forbearing one another in love;

Endeavouring to keep the unity of the Spirit in the bond of peace.

There is one body, and one Spirit, even as ye are called in one hope of your calling;

One Lord, one faith, one baptism,

One God and Father of all, who is above all, and through all, and in you all.

But unto every one of us is given grace according to the measure of the gift of Christ.

Wherefore he saith, When he ascended up on high, he led captivity captive, and gave gifts unto men.

(Now that he ascended, what is it but that he also descended first into the lower parts of the earth?

He that descended is the same also that ascended up far above all heavens, that he might fill all things.)"
Ephesians 4:1-10

If you are faithful in the little, He will give you more. You can have the gifts but not have anointing. You can cast out demons in His name because His name has authority, but to cast out demons because of the anointing, His presence in you is another level. Relational oneness! Jesus had a physician with Him, but it was never used. It was his occupation. He called us to bring His kingdom through His gifts inside of us. He sent us all out! Even with our good works, He won't back us up! Ecumenism will do a lot of works of justice because it is easy to be accepted with them. You can be a man pleaser doing all of that, but you will never be able to please God. Because of mixture, we have infiltrated our faith from the power of God to the power of knowledge and science and carnality. For example: Jesus did not bring glasses with Him in case His power was not working. Jesus did not bring medication in case He was off one day. One way is from religion and the other is from God's government. We need to be determined to walk in His government, submitting to Him – the great Apostle. Here are some signs of dead works of religions: fundraisers, incorporating secular values and ways, agendas of man contrary to the Word, using pagan tradition as an excuse to win the lost, step programs and worldly counseling, planning your future out, working towards retirement, and selling merchandise. These are institutional (Jesus industry), not God's government or Kingdom of God. These are worldly, not from faith! In God's government, He supplies all our needs. We are taken care of, never begging or in need, because everything comes from Jesus. So, if you are struggling then, look at what government you are being loyal too. Nevertheless, He is a miracle maker! In Him, there is no striving.

He is THE way. Not the middle way or the broad way, but HE is the WAY! GOD Himself has set some in the church! All the nine gifts heal the body. The gifts of the Body protect the Body, the joints, supplying the Body, the fivefold is governmental order, and it cannot be mixed with religious systems. If we are mixing it in, it compromises Faith and Truth. Then seducing spirits creep in.

This is what we are ALL called to do: to die, to love, to win the lost, to mortify the deeds of the flesh, to lay down our lives, to pick up our cross, to be a doer of His Word! Rejoice not because you are someone in the Body but because your name is written in the book of life! The carnal church is run under the governments of this World. Jezebel comes in through religion and usurps God's authority and the authority to whom God has ordained and given a mantle, a mandate, and a heavenly vision.

Apostles will need way more grace because of their front line duty! More is always expected from ascension gifts! It costs more. You will be stoned because of them. He gave them, some to be apostles, some to the prophets, evangelists, pastors and teachers to perfect the saints, for the work of the ministry, for the edifying of the Body of Christ! Let's use the gifts for that! It is not about man but the ascension gifts that they have.

"Laying up in store for themselves a good foundation against the time to come, that they may lay hold on eternal life." 1 Timothy 6:19

The twelve Apostles were called by God! God already marked you for what you are supposed to do right when you stepped into the kingdom! Five set positions come from above where all authority comes from, plus administration and helps and government. They are from above. God builds the house by His hands. Religion builds it on the sand with the hands of the flesh. The result of these five specific positions in the Body will bring the unity of faith. It will keep perfecting the Body until we all come into the unity of faith, but people who don't have the ascension gifts are not connected to those who have! Until we all come into the knowledge of who He is and who you are! If you reject them, you are rejecting Christ in them, cutting yourself off from the head of the church, Jesus Himself. So you have an anti-Christ spirit, and you will always be tossed to and fro!

"Now ye are the body of Christ, and members in particular. And God hath set some in the church, first apostles,

secondarily prophets, thirdly teachers, after that miracles, then gifts of healings, helps, governments, diversities of tongues.

Are all apostles? are all prophets? are all teachers? are all workers of miracles?

Have all the gifts of healing? do all speak with tongues? do all interpret?

But covet earnestly the best gifts: and yet shew I unto you a more excellent way." 1 Corinthians 12:27-31

When God says, "He gave gifts to men," that means there is a level of glory, there is a mantle of protection and a constant raising up. It is the person God sets apart to be given to the Body as an ascension gift. Every perfect gift comes from above. A gift is in every believer. It is the Holy Spirit! Then He gave gifts unto men, being the government of God in authority to advance His kingdom. Not religious puppet pastors. Not denominations. Not cults. But authority and keys! He gives a vision and a mandate! He said build on the foundation of the Prophets and the Apostles. Now God is restoring all things for an end time's glorious church to come out of the wilderness leaning on HIM, not on wood, hay, and stubble. On the contrary, the fire of God is burning all that up.

The religious system is anti-Christ. It will always man please, not pleasing God but allowing Jezebel to cut off the head of authority given by God. God's gifts to men stir up religious devils. They are hated by many. They are alone most of the time. Apostles are forerunners, establishing God's government wherever they go. They are sent ones. We are all called to do the works of an evangelist, but apostles take territory.

We are all equal in the Body of Christ as children of God, but in God's governmental kingdom, each person has a specific purpose. There is no equality. We need to recognize them. There is a special authority for those who oversee the sheep! No one is better than the other. It is about God advancing His glory on the Earth. Religion is so self-focused!

Some people will be running around and never submit themselves to the government of God or to people who have specific gifts for them to come into the unity of faith! There is never a real unity of faith among those who don't submit to the ascension gifts set in place by God. What they do is to become an open target to darkness. As well, they never walk in the fullness of the blessing. God's way is the only way.

Apostles and prophets of God will NEVER please people. Ninety percent of the churches out there were not even ordained by God! Until we submit to what and how He is doing it, we will never, ever grow like we should! His mercy and grace have been using these institutions, but God said that He will restore all things. This is what He is doing: building His church.

God told David who He was. Even when man did not see it, He was it. He had that anointing! You must know! Even if people ignore or do not receive from you, don't let that shake you! You may not walk in it fully, but you are IT! Jesus was the lamb of God even before He went to the cross! Don't doubt it!

Jeremiah was a prophet even in his mother's womb! Jeremiah had a mandate from God. So when you are born again, God anoints His government, gives a vision, and sets them apart. In religion, you are always learning, never coming to anything.

These gifts come from above! Not from man! Not from the religious system! Stephen was not even the apostle, but he moved just like one! Why? He submitted to it! If you really want that, you will be stoned like Stephen! Do you really want it? Stephen submitted to God, to the glory, and to governmental leadership. Under these He was able to flow in the same power as one of the twelve. He was not sent in by God's first twelve selections and then his replacement, but he was authority! Twelve is the number of authority: 12 tribes, 12 apostles, 24 elders, together signifying the Government of God. Then 12X12 is 144, and there are a hundred forty-four thousand who come with Jesus with the government on His shoulders that signifies every tongue and every tribe coming with Him. This revelation is from the Holy Spirit.

God will never let anybody humble be deceived! If someone hears from God, that does not make them a prophet. We all are supposed to hear God and be prophetic! If someone starts a church, that does not make him anything. It is about government blueprints from above and not below. The biggest problem is that Satan has had so many transforming themselves into apostles, so many with the Jezebel spirit calling themselves prophets. Even Satan himself has ministers who transform themselves into ministers of righteousness, and these ministers keep on deceiving many. This tactic is so demonic, but we will trust God's true gifts (offices) to the body. Then we see chaos and anarchy all over because Satan is mixing in religion and powerless people who look like sheep, but they are wolves. Just because you've been wolfed, don't despise God's government because that was his intention. Satan is a thief and a liar. Don't throw the baby out with the bath water.

In that, we need to learn how to be content! Find your place. Submit to one another that have what you need. Submit to His ways. Go from a "nothing is good enough attitude" to "all He did is good enough" because your name is written in the book of life! That will bring you right back to no need to compete among gifted people because we all are, but we all have different positions in the Body for raising up, for protection and for advancing. Look at the military. You can see how an army works. Look at the militia, a group of people that engages in rebel or terrorist activities, usually in opposition to a regular army. Most are untrained and end up hurting their own, friendly fire.

God's ways are not our ways! So many people should submit to God's government, and they could be positioned in the Body and grow into His fullness, the same unity of faith, but until submission happens first, that never will happen in their Christian walk. They stay in a religious mindset, the power and the life of God choked out by the python spirit.

The road map of freedom was drawn by God. We need to follow it. At the end of it is the fullness of God being manifested in us and through us! One house, one God who sets and builds; the other, religion (man) sets and builds but on the sand. God can only build on the ROCK.

Let's keep on getting more and more understanding about submission towards those appointed by God and towards the members in the Body.

Read more in the Word and get more revelation: **1 Corinthians 12, Ephesians 4, 1 Timothy 6, 2 Corinthians 11:14-15, Jeremiah 1:4-12, 2 Timothy 2**

THE SPIRIT OF KORAH
By Joe Pinto

Korah, a man of God, an Israelite, a Levite, a set apart one, a leader to the congregation, a worker put in place by God, rose up AGAINST Moses. Moses and Aaron were representing God's Government! With Korah were 250 Israelite men, well-known community leaders who had been appointed members of the council. They came as a group to oppose Moses and Aaron and said to them, "You have gone too far! The whole community is holy, every one of them, and the Lord is with them. Why then do you set yourselves above the Lord's assembly?" When Moses heard this, he fell to his face!

Korah was a man deceived by the vanity of his own heart! Korah really thought in his mind that he was standing up for God and his people, though, in his heart was condemnation because of his lust to be at the top of the platform. This spirit is designed to denounce and take down God's government that is placed in the church as a gift for the saints to build up and bring the church to the full measure of Christ! But wait! Korah believes in Christ?? Korah talks about Christ in himself all the time but never about Christ in others. Is it really about Christ? If you cannot submit to God's government order and body, you are denying Christ. Christ is in you, but He is also in the one in front of you, in the one behind you, in all those who are after the Spirit of God and not after the flesh. The question is, "Are you looking for Christ, or are you focused on man?"

The spirit of Korah will say, "Well, I don't submit to man!" And God says, "It's because you can't see the heart of a man!" If the Corinthian church did not submit to Paul's gift set in place by God, they would have perished! They were ready to go fornicate with people in their own family! Why does this happen and even happen in the church today? Because there is no order from heaven in the church. We have leaders, we have pastors, we have ushers, we have fundraisers, we have coffee and tea, but we don't have set and sent ones. The majority of the church have no clue of the authentic fivefold ministry. Why? Does God not want to send his government to the American church? No! You know why? Because the American church does not want it! They just want to know that Christ is in them. They think they are blameless in God's sight, and they are going to heaven.

This is not the Gospel! Jesus didn't die for us to pretend! He died for us to know Him and to be restored as sons and daughters. The remnant is set apart from mainstream Christianity. They shall know him and receive the gift of God's government so that they can grow into the full stature of Christ. God has made and designed these gifts for them. O precious remnant, no longer being tossed to and fro by every wind of doctrine! Korah is tossed to and fro by every wind of doctrine! Why? Because it's doing everything it can to draw attention to self, to make its own ministry, to be the next hip Christian entertainment of the day.

Korah believes that Jesus died for his sins; therefore, he is holy and perfect before God, and because of this, he doesn't need to receive from anyone else. He doesn't need to assemble together with the saints because he's got it all in him, but Korah is a presumptuous fool! Why? Because he has failed to observe and come into agreement with the very things that were set by God to protect him from losing all the things inside of him. Korah says that God will never leave him or forsake him but doesn't realize that he can leave God and forsake God! Korah professes all the truth, and even the truth that you speak, though he does not really believe it all, he believes it for you: To appease you! To please you! In the end, to cease you! To his own deception! So that you may become an audience member to his ministry or become a giving partner to support himself. In Korah's life, it seems all about God, though it's all about him. Korah will tear down any leadership of any kind, because it believes it's a free for all. It will tell you, "Yes, go all out for the Lord," but it is out of order, losing mindfulness of Satan's demons entering his own life. In Numbers, Korah accuses Moses of the very thing he is guilty of. He calls Moses prideful, lording over others, or self seeking; meanwhile, Korah is guilty of these things, even though Korah has such a good front put up, such a good false character, such a powerful display. Don't be deceived! Korah is a showman, so much to the point that he gets real anointed men and woman of God to question their own walk and identity.

We must have sharp discernment or else we will not identify those who say they are what they are but are another person inside. Therefore, it shall deceive us with its false outward person. Meanwhile, the inward demons of Korah are feeding us their spiritual garbage. Pay attention! You may think she or he is on fire for the Lord, though they are ready any day to use you and abuse you and to make merchandise of you that they may sell you their false Christianity. The root of Korah is this: Easy believism. Telling Moses, "... but we're all Holy!" Moses said, "Let me show you who's Holy! When we both enter the presence of my Father, who will still be standing? The one who only believes or the one who knows Him?" Today, Korah and Moses stand before the Lord, but only one will stand before the Lord with his works burned by fire and the other a recompense for glory and riches in the heavenly realm to come!

Don't be deceived by this spirit that you would become a maverick or a lone ranger. Do not rob yourself of what God has set in the church for you. These Korahs are out there in the majority church. Or they are out there in the lonely caves that they would take you in and make you just like them: to rebel against the Lord himself.

Jesus said I am the Word! So what does that mean? If you come against God's Word and order, you are actually coming against God Himself. Don't become a Korah and have your works be burned by fire, to have your altar and incense to the

Lord shut down and covered up that you would be veiled from the Father again.

When Joshua led the Israelites into the land of Canaan, the sons of Levi were the only Israelite tribe that received cities but were not allowed to be land owners because the Lord Himself was to be their inheritance. Will God have to put you on the shelf so that you can learn to covet Him instead of your ministry? May God have mercy on you, so that you may be counted worthy to have Him and lands (the inheritance) on this earth, in this time.

Korah will be swallowed up by the Earth and its fornication, but God's government and Body will live on.

Where do you stand today? Serve God or serve Baal!

Read more in the Word and get more revelation: **Numbers 15, Numbers 16, Numbers 17, Numbers 18, Joshua 13:33, Ephesians 4:1-16**

4
AWAKENING WHAT WAS BURIED

AWAKENING THE GIFTS

& PRODUCING THE FRUITS OF THE SPIRIT

"Now concerning spiritual gifts, brethren,
I would not have you ignorant." 1 Corinthians 12:1

Awakening the gifts buried inside you
+ growing the fruits of the Spirit = Explosion!

Let's start with the gifts: [Never forget this!]

Gifts are NOT for one man but are for EVERYONE, for you, for me, for all of us!

Church, God is saying, "Do not neglect the gifts of the Spirit. Desire them, covet them, and receive them."

Now, more than ever, God is going to pour out His spirit on all flesh, on His bride, and on His church. We need only to desire, receive, honor, practice and perfect them. Why? So that we can destroy the works of Satan, and so that we can bless the body, edify one another, and draw people to Jesus. These gifts are not just for you but for others. Many are using God's gifts to exalt oneself, but let's take hold of these gifts and destroy the works of darkness!

Ask, ask, ask for spiritual gifts!

Matthew 7:11 says, **"If ye then, being evil, know how to give good gifts unto your children, how much more shall your Father which is in heaven give good things to them that ask him?"**

Diversities of gifts are placed in you: **Romans 12:6-21 / 1 Corinthians 12**

Receive and activate the gifts of the Spirit.

"Do not neglect the GIFT that is in you, which was given to you by prophecy with the laying on of the hands of the eldership." 1 Timothy 4:14

Now is the time for those who have the gifts of the Spirit to grow up and activate them. Today is the day for those who don't have them to receive them as well. We need these weapons of warfare. The gifts are for the unbelievers so they can believe. Paul clearly says, "I don't come with wise, vain, jangling, enticing words but in power and demonstrations of the Holy Spirit." Brother Paul knew how important these gifts are.

We need to stop talking about it and start walking in HIM. We need to know who we are, what we have, and how to use these mighty weapons. Covet the best gift, Brothers!

"DO NOT BE IGNORANT ABOUT THE GIFTS."
1 Corinthians 12

THE NINE GIFTS OF THE SPIRIT:

- **REVELATORY GIFTS**: words of wisdom, words of knowledge, discerning of spirits.

- **POWER AND DEMONSTRATION GIFTS**: gifts of faith, gifts of healing, gifts of miracles.

- **UTTERANCE GIFTS**: prophecy, diverse kinds of tongues, interpretation of tongues.

IF YOU ARE PART OF THE BODY,
YOU ARE GIFTED JUST LIKE THE HEAD, JESUS.
HE GAVE GIFTS UNTO ALL MEN.

"Praying for us with much entreaty that we would receive the gift, and take upon us the fellowship of ministering to the saints." 2 Corinthians 8: 4

God is raising up men and women as a gift to the body so that we can grow into the maturity in the faith. God is bringing forth all the gifts; none is better than the other. Seek what gift you have and that will be the highest place you can ever be. We must submit one to another, giving honor to Christ. No one is esteemed higher than the other, but we give honor to one another, rooted and grounded in love. **"I prophesy that every joint out of order in the Body will be put in place."** God is bringing the true fivefold ministries and the Body of Christ together.

WE ARE ORDINARY PEOPLE
WITH EXTRAORDINARY GIFTS
Acts 6: 2-8; 1 Corinthians 1: 25-31

Very anointed and with the character of Christ: That is the true disciple of Jesus. It is time to reap good fruits. Delight yourself as you read the book of Galatians, Chapter 5.

God is calling us to Himself – the only one who can produce fruit in us as we are connected to the vine. He is the vine. We are the branches. It is God who gives the increase if we have fruit. He wants the fruit of our labor to be the fruits of righteousness, obedience, love, and so forth.

In this passage, I will expose and show you that you are a tree of life, but if there is no life in you, you cannot give life to others.

Those trees that don't produce fruit are either: 1) plucked up; 2) cursed; or 3) rejected. Let us be the type of tree that produces fruit that is pleasant and that is desirable. God has not called us to judge, but He has called us to inspect the fruit of others so we will know who is in the faith and who to trust. In that way, we will not be abused, misused, or tossed to and fro. The fruit of the truth is the ultimate gift of the Holy Spirit.

Let us examine ourselves first of all that we may know Him. Staying connected to Him is the only way to bear the fruit of the Spirit. Beware: There is other fruit. The devil has his own fruit stuck right in the middle, and we must continually be trimming it away. Bad fruit is the fruit that cannot remain. What fruit are you bearing?

We have seen so many anointed people with very little fruit. What the World wants to see from us is that we really come from HIM, FROM HIS VINE:

"But the fruit of the Spirit is love, joy, peace, longsuffering, gentleness, goodness, faith, meekness, temperance!" Galatians 5:22-23

5
AUTHORITY OF THE BELIEVER

It is time to walk in the authority that He gave us. Who am I?

YOU ARE THE ANOINTED ONE.

Now with the fruits and gifts of the Spirit together, it's time to walk in HIS authority.

This is the time. This is the day. Be of good cheer. He has given us AUTHORITY OVER ALL DEMONS and AUTHORITY TO CURE DISEASES **(Luke 9:1)**. With authority and power we will command the unclean spirits, and they will come out **(Luke 4:36)**. He has given us authority to go in His name, to heal the sick, cleanse the lepers, raise the dead, cast out demons. He has given us the commandment to go into all the world and to preach the gospel to every person

42

(Matthew 10:5-8). He has given us the authority to bring HIS KINDGOM DOWN ON EARTH JUST AS IT IS IN HEAVEN! Glory! You got it. Use it! Preach the WORD (2 Timothy 4:2-5). Take your place and go!

He called all of us UNTO HIM (Matthew 10:1), and He gave us POWER against unclean spirits, to cast them out of ourselves and out of His church, and to heal ALL manner of sickness and ALL manner of disease. He said to us to PREACH THE KINGDOM OF HEAVEN IS AT HAND. He commanded us, every BELIEVER, to show off HIS POWER! The world is waiting for the manifestation of the Sons of God! Let's go out there and do our job! He placed His authority on us. He placed His anointing on us. Let's use it!

"The Spirit of the Lord GOD is upon me; because the LORD hath anointed me to preach good tidings unto the meek; he hath sent me to bind up the brokenhearted, to proclaim liberty to the captives, and the opening of the prison to them that are bound; To proclaim the acceptable year of the LORD, and the day of vengeance of our God; to comfort all that mourn; To appoint unto them that mourn in Zion, to give unto them beauty for ashes, the oil of joy for mourning, the garment of praise for the spirit of heaviness; that they might be called trees of righteousness, the planting of the LORD, that he might be glorified." Isaiah 61:1-3

BINDING THE STRONGMAN

WE HAVE AUTHORITY IN CHRIST JESUS

Army, let's BIND the strong man to take his spoils.
(Luke 11: 22)

The "strong man" is Satan who possesses or works in human beings by means of his wicked spirits. Satan is as clearly a person as the Lord Jesus Christ is a Person! The Lord Jesus Christ dwells in those He redeems by His Spirit. He imparts to them the very life of the Son of God, thus making them children of God. In the same way, the prince of darkness possesses or controls the fallen race of Adam **(1 John 5: 19)**. The Apostle John says that he is "the spirit that now worketh in the sons of disobedience" **(Ephesians 2:2)**; the Apostle John emphatically says, "He that doeth sin is of the devil" **(1 John 3: 8)**, a partaker of his evil nature; while James writes, "Jealousy and faction...is earthly, natural, DEVILISH" **(James 3:14-15)**. The Lord describes the strong man's attitude when in possession of the man: "FULLY ARMED" HE GUARDS HIS COURTS and keeps his goods safe **(Luke 11:21)**! How true this is of all who are in the kingdom of darkness! Paul the Apostle describes one way in which the strong man guards his house when he writes, "The god of this world hath blinded the thoughts of the unbelieving, that the light of the gospel should not dawn upon them." **2 Corinthians 4:4**

Until we recognize that the "fully armed" strong man is behind all darkness of thought and blindness to the Gospel, we cannot do much toward bringing men out of the power of darkness into the kingdom of God's dear Son. Until we take heed to the Lord's warning to FIRST, "bind the strong man," the attempts we make to "spoil his goods" will only enrage him and enable him to strengthen his armor and guard his palace in peace.

One way is to start hating sin in our lives. The more we purify ourselves, the weaker this evil spirit will be. There is "ANOTHER MAN STRONGER THAN HE!" The Lord says, "When a 'Stronger than he shall come upon him,' then 'He takes from him his whole armor wherein he trusted, and divides his spoils'" **(Luke 11:22)**. The Lord was talking about JESUS; now JESUS IS IN US. We are crucified with Christ so we have died to sin **(Romans 6:6)** and died to the world belonging to the evil one. We refuse to let sin reign in our mortal bodies. To tamper with sin of any kind will quench the power of the Holy Spirit in us and only by the Spirit of God can we "bind" the operations of the strongman around us. We have to set our choice to serve God, not sin, at all cost. We must refuse to let sin reign. Joined to Him in Spirit, we shall not fulfill the lust of our flesh! There will be no room for this kind of activity in us and around us. The Bible says in **1 John 4:4: "You, dear children, are from God and have overcome them, because the one who is in you is greater than the one who is in the world."**

SHANE W ROESSIGER

The Bible also declares that: **"I will give you the keys of the kingdom of heaven; whatever you bind on earth will be bound in heaven, and whatever you loose on earth will be loosed in heaven." Matthew 16:19**

Glory, glory, glory! Purified by the blood of Jesus and with nothing in common with the works of the flesh, we are ready to open our mouths, by faith, and start binding the strongman and loosing the Kingdom of heaven on earth! Hallelujah! We are overcomers!

The 12 Strongmen	The Symptoms	The Scriptures
1. Jealousy	Rage, Anger, Suspicion, Murder, Revenge, Competition, Vengeance	Numbers 5: 11-15 Proverbs 6: 34-35
2. Lying	Falsehood, Flattery, Stubbornness, Right all the time	Ezekiel 12:24 Jeremiah 23: 14-16
3. Familiar Spirits	Divination, Mediums, Spells, Horoscopes, Occult	Deuteronomy 18: 10-12 1 Samuel 28:7
4. Perverse	Homosexuality, Lust, Pornography, Hates God, Falsifies the Word	Isaiah 19: 14 Proverbs 14:2 Acts 13:10

5. Harlotry	Whoredom, Prostitution, Soap Operas	Hosea 4:12 Ezekiel 16: 28-35
6. Heaviness	Gluttony, Rejection, Guilt, Weight Problems, Grief, Self-pity, Depression, Hopelessness, Cutting, Hurts Oneself	Isaiah 61:3
7. Infirmity	Sickness	Luke 13:11
8. Deaf and Dumb	Seizures, Epilepsy, Anorexia, Suicide, Craziness, Mental Illness	Mark 9: 17-25 Matthew 17: 14-15
9. Fear	Torment, Terror, Nightmares, Phobias	Job 4:14
10. Pride	Wrath, Control, Contention, Self-righteousness, Self-seeking, Fighting	Proverbs 16:18
11. Bondage	All addictions, Spirit of slavery	Romans 8:15
12. Antichrist	Religious spirit, Anything that comes against God	1 John 4:3

FINDING AGAINST
THE JEZEBEL SPIRIT

JEZEBEL: THE EVIL SPIRIT SENT TO KILL THE
PROPHETS AND THE APOSTOLIC IN THE CHURCH

"And unto the angel of the church in Thyatira write; These things saith the Son of God, who hath his eyes like unto a flame of fire, and his feet are like fine brass; I know thy works, and charity, and service, and faith, and thy patience, and thy works; and the last to be more than the first. Notwithstanding I have a few things against thee, because thou sufferest that woman Jezebel, which calleth herself a prophetess, to teach and to seduce my servants to commit fornication, and to eat things sacrificed unto idols. And I gave her space to repent of her fornication; and she repented not. Behold, I will cast her into a bed, and them that commit adultery with her into great tribulation, except they repent of their deeds." Revelation 2:18-22

We have seen throughout the Bible that every time God sent His prophets to the land, there was a spirit trying to shut down His voice. Remember John the Baptist? How about Elijah? Her name is JEZEBEL!* Her main purpose is to shut down the prophetic voice in the church. When Jesus spoke in **Revelation 2:19-29,** He was speaking to the leaders of the church because as the anointing runs from the head down so does the entrance of unclean spirits such as Jezebel. Her main

48

purpose is to control the leaders and God's people so God cannot move.

She wants to grieve the Holy Spirit. When this spirit comes into the church, she has the leaders teach on the Jezebel spirit. Actually, this is her trick because everyone starts to look at each other to see if they have one of her characteristics when the main focus – the leaders – are the ones being led by the Jezebel spirit.

Then walls are put up – division and confusion start happening in the church. This beast becomes more powerful. Unity and freedom will kill this giant, but repentance must come first from the head down. Leaders are responsible to bind and loose this beast, but when we let her in, the heaven's become brass. This spirit will come and seduce leaders. She is not concerned as much about the sheep although she will try to work through them as well. She knows the damage. She will do it from the top.

We must cover one another, but we must cover our leader first. In the Old Testament, Jezebel wanted to destroy the prophet, Elijah **(1 Kings 19:2).** In the New Testament, the same happened to John the Baptist when they asked for his head **(Mark 6:24)**. So, If Jesus Himself has rebuked the church for the Jezebel spirit in Revelation, and the Old Testament is a shadow of what is to come, watch out for false fire: controlling pastors and leaders who are content to be the only voice, the only teacher, the only one prophesying. Beware! As anointed as this leader might be, this leader might be dancing with

Jezebel!

Jezebel's function is to control. She controls with words and manipulation. Many times, the leaders make the members work for them by saying, "THIS is the house of GOD." That's how they get you to labor for them. "God's house," they always say. The Bible tells us that serving God is growing up into what God has for you, your gift and assignment, but this spirit keeps everyone in the pews. She tells you that her congregation is the best one in the world and that everyone else should be there, too. However, that body never grows spiritually. Children are tossed to and fro because they are getting whatever the pastor tries to serve them, but it is not meat. Remember: I am exposing Jezebel; I am not coming against any child of God nor against His beautiful bride, but against the spirit that my Lord is telling me to reveal through these dreams and visions. In the book of Malachi, it is written, **"Will a man rob God through His tithes and offerings"** (Malachi 3:8).

A Jezebel spirit makes YOU the thief when the leaders talk about tithing. For example, God is talking to the priest, the leader of the Church, who makes everyone bring his tithe to the storehouse: the church, the building. The priest [the leaders] were spending the money and eating the goods. They were not taking care of the poor and the widows. This spirit will twist God's words and manipulate the sheep, never allowing the gifts in the House to operate. How does this spirit seduce us? Through luxury and vanities. When you go into these places, everyone says how awesome the leader is, how beautiful the building is, how great the ministry is. It is all about them, about their own kingdom, NOT about Jesus. Little Jesus, big leader.

This spirit of Jezebel commits adultery with the system of the world and demands respect, but we know that God's kingdom is opposite from the World system. God said this spirit is wrongly seducing and teaching His servants.

The church of Thyatira represents the world or religious system that allows anointing to make covenants with worldly systems **(Revelation 2:18)**.

1 John 2: 15-16: "Love not the world, neither the things that are in the world. If any man love the world, the love of the father is not in Him, for all that is in the World, the lust of the flesh and the lust of the eye and the pride of life, is not the Father, but is of the World." Revelation 2:18

James 4:4: "You adulterous people. Don't you know that friendship with the world is hatred toward God? Anyone who chooses to be a friend of the world becomes an enemy of God."

When you yoke up with unbelievers, you turn the House of God into the House of Dagon and idols **(1 Samuel 5)**. What happened to the sayings of Jesus? He said in **Matthew 20:25-28, "But Jesus called them to Himself and said, 'You know that the rulers of the Gentiles lord it over them, and those who are great exercise authority over them. Yet it shall not be so among** you; but whoever desires to become great among you, let him be your servant. And whoever desires to be first among you, let him be your slave— just as the Son of Man did not come to be served, but to serve, and to give His life a ransom for many.'"

Who do you think you are? Get off your high horse! Divorce Jezebel.* Clean your church. Smash your golden calf. Repent and start to serve God's people. There are several places in this region that are dancing with and dating Jezebel. God says, "I am jealous. I am lovesick." **(Ezekiel 8)**. RETURN, RETURN, RETURN TO ME." Time is short. Game time is over. God is taking back His bride from every harlot. Release your control and your manipulation. God will reveal you openly. You have had many warnings in night dreams and visions. Do not lie. Boldness comes from God. This region will be God's, not man's. Loose, loose, loose! Face God! Change your ways! Stop making empty promises: Your words have become powerless. Repent and return to your first love, or I [Jesus] will remove my candlestick from you, says the Lord **(Revelation 2:1-7)**.

We pray that you will stir up the gifts of the discerning of spirits inside of you **(1 Corinthians 12:10)** and that your eyes will be opened to see what the Spirit is showing you.

"That the God of our Lord Jesus Christ, the Father of glory, may give unto you the spirit of wisdom and revelation in the

knowledge of him: The eyes of your understanding being enlightened; that ye may know what is the hope of his calling, and what the riches of the glory of his inheritance in the saints." Ephesians 1:17-18

Note: The reason God is exposing this beast is that His children are bound and controlled and cannot grow into their Kingdom assignments. They can never grow up and become what God has ordained for them. Ask the Lord to give you the discerning of spirits so you will see if you have been led by the Holy Spirit or by the spirit of Jezebel and repent. It is a new beginning for you today!

*When we were referring to Jezebel, the feminine pronouns were used. However this spirit does not have a gender.

SCATTERED & GATHERED

"Woe be unto the pastors that destroy and scatter the sheep of my pasture! saith the LORD. Therefore thus saith the LORD God of Israel against the pastors that feed my people; Ye have scattered my flock, and driven them away, and have not visited them: behold, I will visit upon you the evil of your doings, saith the LORD.

And I will gather the remnant of my flock out of all countries whither I have driven them, and will bring them again to their folds; and they shall be fruitful and increase.

And I will set up shepherds over them which shall feed them: and they shall fear no more, nor be dismayed, neither shall they be lacking, saith the LORD.

Behold, the days come, saith the LORD, that I will raise unto David a righteous Branch, and a King shall reign and prosper, and shall execute judgment and justice in the earth.

In his days Judah shall be saved, and Israel shall dwell safely: and this is his name whereby he shall be called, THE LORD OUR RIGHTEOUSNESS.

Therefore, behold, the days come, saith the LORD, that they shall no more say, The LORD liveth, which brought up the children of Israel out of the land of Egypt;

But, The LORD liveth, which brought up and which led the seed of the house of Israel out of the north country, and from all countries whither I had driven them; and they shall dwell in their own land.

Mine heart within me is broken because of the prophets; all my bones shake; I am like a drunken man, and like a man whom wine hath overcome, because of the LORD, and because of the words of his holiness.

For the land is full of adulterers; for because of swearing the land mourneth; the pleasant places of the wilderness are dried up, and their course is evil, and their force is not right.

For both prophet and priest are profane; yea, in my house have I found their wickedness, saith the LORD.

[12] Wherefore their way shall be unto them as slippery ways in the darkness: they shall be driven on, and fall therein: for I will bring evil upon them, even the year of their visitation, saith the LORD.

And I have seen folly in the prophets of Samaria; they prophesied in Baal, and caused my people Israel to err.

I have seen also in the prophets of Jerusalem an horrible thing: they commit adultery, and walk in lies: they strengthen also the hands of evildoers, that none doth return from his wickedness; they are all of them unto me as Sodom, and the inhabitants thereof as Gomorrah.

Therefore thus saith the LORD of hosts concerning the prophets; Behold, I will feed them with wormwood, and make them drink the water of gall: for from the prophets of Jerusalem is profaneness gone forth into all the land.

Thus saith the LORD of hosts, Hearken not unto the words of the prophets that prophesy unto you: they make you vain: they speak a vision of their own heart, and not out of the mouth of the LORD.

They say still unto them that despise me, The LORD hath said, Ye shall have peace; and they say unto every one that walketh after the imagination of his own heart, No evil shall come upon you.

For who hath stood in the counsel of the LORD, and hath perceived and heard his word? who hath marked his word, and heard it?

Behold, a whirlwind of the LORD is gone forth in fury, even a grievous whirlwind: it shall fall grievously upon the head of the wicked.

The anger of the LORD shall not return, until he have executed, and till he have performed the thoughts of his heart: in the latter days ye shall consider it perfectly.

I have not sent these prophets, yet they ran: I have not spoken to them, yet they prophesied.

But if they had stood in my counsel, and had caused my people to hear my words, then they should have turned them from their evil way, and from the evil of their doings.

Am I a God at hand, saith the LORD, and not a God afar off?

Can any hide himself in secret places that I shall not see him? saith the LORD. Do not I fill heaven and earth? saith the LORD.

I have heard what the prophets said, that prophesy lies in my name, saying, I have dreamed, I have dreamed.

How long shall this be in the heart of the prophets that prophesy lies? yea, they are prophets of the deceit of their own heart;

Which think to cause my people to forget my name by their dreams which they tell every man to his neighbour, as their fathers have forgotten my name for Baal.

The prophet that hath a dream, let him tell a dream; and he that hath my word, let him speak my word faithfully. What is the chaff to the wheat? saith the LORD.

Is not my word like as a fire? saith the LORD; and like a hammer that breaketh the rock in pieces?

Therefore, behold, I am against the prophets, saith the LORD, that steal my words every one from his neighbour.

Behold, I am against the prophets, saith the LORD, that use their tongues, and say, He saith.

Behold, I am against them that prophesy false dreams, saith the LORD, and do tell them, and cause my people to err by their lies, and by their lightness; yet I sent them not, nor commanded them: therefore they shall not profit this people at all, saith the LORD.

And when this people, or the prophet, or a priest, shall ask thee, saying, What is the burden of the LORD? thou shalt then say unto them, What burden? I will even forsake you, saith the LORD.

And as for the prophet, and the priest, and the people, that shall say, The burden of the LORD, I will even punish that man and his house.

Thus shall ye say every one to his neighbour, and every one to his brother, What hath the LORD answered? and, What hath the LORD spoken?

And the burden of the LORD shall ye mention no more: for every man's word shall be his burden; for ye have perverted the words of the living God, of the LORD of hosts our God.

Thus shalt thou say to the prophet, What hath the LORD answered thee? and, What hath the LORD spoken?

But since ye say, The burden of the LORD; therefore thus saith the LORD; Because ye say this word, The burden of the LORD, and I have sent unto you, saying, Ye shall not say, The burden of the LORD;

Therefore, behold, I, even I, will utterly forget you, and I will forsake you, and the city that I gave you and your fathers, and cast you out of my presence:

And I will bring an everlasting reproach upon you, and a perpetual shame, which shall not be forgotten." Jeremiah 23

God is exposing the wolves that are scattering the sheep. The goats and the sheep are being separated by God Himself, but the wolves are scattering them all. If Satan can turn the real shepherds into hirelings, it is a demonic strategy: It will scatter them from eating and from being led by the true shepherd. He uses fear and points out things, but He is a liar. He is after the little ones.

If you don't gather with Him, you are scattering. Wolves have been feeding God's sheep. Evil spirits are finding place because they are not being continually filled by the Spirit of God. False teaching and false doctrines are causing many sheep to fall into the ditch, to walk in darkness, and to drink from muddy waters.

They write books from Baal. They write messages from Baal. They prophesy lies. They are actors who dress up for a party. They are not sent by God.

The unbelieving Christians became wolves. The unbelieving Baptist or anybody that does not believe on the Holy Spirit became wolves. The unbelieving Jews were stirring the Gentiles. It does not matter which denomination you are from; if you change any of His Word, you became a scatterer! They make the minds of the little sheep evil. Then they start questioning, rebelling, taking scriptures and twisting it to fit in their denomination, their doctrine and their pernicious ways. So instead of gathering them around the shepherd, they are scattering them. The shepherd goes in one direction: One way! He will bring to the sword those who scatter His little sheep. Cities are being divided into truth or religion, compromise or loyalty to the truth. Part will go after the religious; part will go after Him! We are One Spirit, One accord, One fold following One shepherd!

Not everybody can open the door of the fold. Only those with Jesus! Apostles and real prophets are porters to the door. We must eat from green pastures, drinking living water! We either are for Him, the good chief shepherd, or against Him. If we are for Him, we are for the sheep!

Do you want the Truth? Do you believe the Truth? Real sheep will not follow man without Jesus or man without the Holy Spirit. The Holy Spirit guides us into all Truth; it guides us into all of Jesus. There are many actors dressed up as shepherds, but they are ministers of ministry, of scattering instead of gathering. They seem to be for Him, but they are really against Him, full of hidden motives.

There is only one door to the fold: the Holy Spirit! The goats will follow the stranger because they will just walk after his voice. Just focus on the sheep and on the good shepherd. He will separate those that look the same, but they are not. They are those who dress themselves as sheep and shepherds but are ravishing wolves! Many false shepherds are really angels of light!

Heresies cause division, but God will not allow His sheep to be divided as He divides goats, as He scatters the wolves. He will expose the prophets of Baal. He will make sure you don't follow any of them. A house divided by man can't stand, but a fold divided by God will remain forever!

Many will hear again that the voice of the bride is the voice of the remnant. God will cause them to come out of captivity back to the fold of the good shepherd. He will bring health, and He will cure the little sheep. He will reveal unto them the abundance of peace and truth. He will cause them to return to the fold and will build them as at the first. They will hear the voice of joy, the voice of the bridegroom, the voice of the bride. The voice of the bridegroom is the voice of the good shepherd.

"So many thieves and robbers will enter not by the door into the sheepfold but will climb up some other way. To get to God's little sheep, you have to come through the door. Jesus is the door of the sheep, and He only opens it up for those who have the fierce heart of Peter. "Peter, feed, take care, watch over My sheep..."

Satan is out there to get them. He is thief and a robber, always trying to climb that wall. He finds hirelings. What should have been a divine choice, Satan turned into a job/career. When they see the wolf coming, they leave the sheep and flee. They don't care about them. They are all for themselves! For their ministry! For their lives! There are so many scattered sheep because of them.

At the same time, there are so many, many real Godly shepherds zealous for God's sheep that go out there, leave the fold after the wolves, forgetting that wolves walk in packs. As you are trying to kill one, many others are attacking the fold. The good shepherd does not go after wolves! They SEE them coming! They don't leave the fold, not even for a second. They protect the gates! They protect the sheep! They lay down their lives for them. Their eyes are on the sheep, constantly. It is a nonstop, 24/7 care!

The shepherd is always communicating with the sheep. They keep hearing their voices because it sounds just like the Father's voice, and there is no way to follow any other. The shepherd knows them by name, knows their weakness, also their strength. The shepherd knows who are his and who are not. No thieves, no robbers, no wolves can get into it because the gate is always closed. The watchmen are set on the wall. No way for them to climb it!

Jesus is the door of the sheep. If He has opened up that door to you, make sure you don't open it up to any other..."
Marlene Roessiger

"Then said Jesus unto them again, Verily, verily, I say unto you, I am the door of the sheep. But he that entereth in by the door is the shepherd of the sheep. All that ever came before me are thieves and robbers: but the sheep did not hear them."
John 10:7-8

6
WAKE UP CALL

YOU ARE THE GIANTS IN THIS LAND
The price of the anointing in your life: Everything!

1) SEPARATE YOURSELF: "COME OUT FROM AMONG THEM" (2 Corinthians 6: 14-18)

God is calling His people out from the World system, the world religions, the world's compromising, unrighteous ways that seem right to a man, but in the end, it is death. We cannot sit at the table of devils and sit at the table of the Lord: two kingdoms, two masters. One serves self – the other serves others. One is pagan traditions, religions and compromise – the other is truth, righteousness, purity, wholeness and holiness. Little foxes spoil the vine; a little leaven will leaven the lump. Come out into truth. Quit listening to the voices in the World that lead you to fear, self, and the broad way. There is only ONE way: The holy highway through the blood and the purging of our own thinking, breaking the mindset of what we think is okay. Clearly, the Word of God says to judge yourself, not by those around you but by the Word of Truth. Then you will be counted worthy of your inheritance. God's grace and power are here to obtain all that He desires for us, but we must submit every area of our lives to Him so that we can see his kingdom manifested on this earth **(Matthew 6:22-24; Ephesians 5:6-18)**.

2) BE READY TO PAY THE PRICE: YOUR LIFE

Jesus paid the price for our sins. Don't forget that he bought you with a price and that He will have His glory in you. There is a price for you to pay also: your life. God is raising up true voices in the land whether we like it or not. Jesus said to deny yourself and follow Him. God is saying that it is time to expose the apostasy: the blind and deceitful workers of iniquity luring many away from the Truth. Are you ready? For with the truth comes fire, testing, trials, and purging your will. You continue to have your ears tickled with these apostasy rising soothsayers, promising you that you should keep your life, when Jesus said, "Give me your life." They are liars, clouds without water. When you decide to follow the way of righteousness, He will give you all you need in due time. Do not be deceived. The true Gospel of Jesus Christ is not cheap: It will cost you everything.

"What good will it be for a man if he gains the whole world, yet loose his soul? Or what can a man give in exchange for his soul?" Matthew 16:26

"The man who loves his life will lose it, while the man who hates his life in this world will keep it for eternal life." John 12:25

3) MAKE A COMMITMENT TO PREACH THE FULLNESS OF THE GOSPEL

"And I am sure that, when I come unto you, I shall come in the fullness of the blessing of the gospel of Christ." Romans 15:29

Desire to be totally led by the Spirit and to preach the gospel of Jesus Christ with boldness and not timidity. We must never grieve the Holy Spirit. We have made churches so organized and structured that we have left out the great, "I AM," but, today, the Lord is back in the house. The fear of the Lord is the beginning of wisdom. The congregation's purpose is not to make someone's name great. We will bridge the gap together. Signs and wonders will follow the Word of Truth. It is your calling to speak THE TRUTH in love. The Word of God is not an opinion or a way. It is THE way.

Right now, apostles, prophets, evangelists, pastors, and teachers are being raised up. You are one of them! Seek the Lord and ask for a revelation of your calling, of your destiny.

The world is waiting, not only for you to bring the good news, but to demonstrate the power of the kingdom of God. It is time for a demonstration of the power of WHAT YOU ARE PREACHING!

"And my speech and my preaching was not with enticing words of man's wisdom, but in demonstration of the Spirit and of power." 1 Corinthians 2:4

We have a lot of "Esthers" — women and men - soaked in the oil of His presence. Guess what? You are more than ready! Get out of the tub. Get out and serve the King! Get out and bring others to the tub so they can be changed, delivered, and freed. Do what Jesus has commanded, "Go into all the world and preach the gospel to all nations!" This commandment is for all believers. Maybe God is not expecting you to go and have big crusades or go to the street corner with a megaphone, but you have a realm and a circle of people you communicate with — that you need to invite to come and eat at the Lord's table.

Why?

- **Because of love.**
- **Jesus died a horrific death for them. He desires that none shall perish.**
- **It's not about you or me, but Him.**

Paul was speaking to all believers because he is saying, "DO THE WORKS of an evangelist." He did not say, "Evangelist, go evangelize." Here it is:

"Preach the word! Be ready in season and out of season. Convince, rebuke, exhort, with all longsuffering and teaching. For the time will come when they will not endure sound doctrine, but according to their own desires, because they have itching ears, they will heap up for themselves teachers; and they will turn their ears away from the truth, and be turned aside to fables. But you be watchful in all things, endure afflictions, do the work of an evangelist, fulfill your ministry." 2 Timothy 4:2-5

Every disciple went and preached, healed, and delivered them wherever they were. Come on. People are dying around us. His yoke is easy and His burden is light. Do it His way and see how right and awesome you feel. Faith without works is dead. The works that God wants, He demonstrated them through His son. We are an army, not a social club, and the chief is God, and we must all fight. We are a battleship, not a cruise line. Jesus has commanded us what to do. He delegates authority, and now He told me to tell you, **GO**!

"Then Jesus went about all the cities and villages, teaching in their synagogues, preaching the gospel of the kingdom, and healing every sickness and every disease among the people. But when He saw the multitudes, He was moved with compassion for them, because they were weary and scattered, like sheep

having no shepherd. Then He said to His disciples, "The harvest truly is plentiful, but the laborers are few. Therefore pray the Lord of the harvest to send out laborers into His harvest." Matthew 9:35-38

4) MAKE THE HOLY SPIRIT OUR ETERNAL PARTNER.

In these last days, we will see Christians walking in the Spirit and with the Spirit of God. We will see the fruits of the Spirit, the gifts of the Spirit, and the power of the Spirit of God working together. That is when the explosion happens. Everyone who desires to be touched by God will be touched by God. We can never tell the Holy Spirit what to do. We are His servants. We have to submit to Him. He is not here to serve us. He is our master. He calls the shots. This is the shift in the Body. It is available to you: a pioneering anointing to bring the Body back together, to fix the broken places, to repair the walls, and to clean the temple. We know that you will face much persecution, but we pray for the fullness of joy as we receive one hundredfold in this time. Come alongside, make your name in heaven known, and join us in building something that will remain after being tested by fire.

"Every man's work shall be made manifest: for the day shall declare it, because it shall be revealed by fire; and the fire shall try every man's work of what sort it is." 1 Corinthians 3:13

"But speaking the truth in love, may grow up into him in all things, which is the head, even Christ: From whom the whole body fitly joined together and compacted by that which every joint supplieth, according to the effectual working in the measure of every part, maketh increase of the body unto the edifying of itself in love." Ephesians 4:15-16

5) OBEY THE GREAT COMMISSION: MARK 16:15-20

A church is not a Kingdom church if it is not using the gifts and the power of the Holy Spirit in order to reach a lost soul. Equipped and empowered, the members of the Body of Christ will boldly go out to obey the great commandment given in **Mark 16:15-20**.

"And he said unto them, 'Go ye into all the world, and preach the gospel to every creature. He that believeth and is baptized shall be saved; but he that believeth not shall be damned. And **these signs shall follow** them that believe; **In my name shall they cast out devils; they shall speak with new tongues; They shall take up serpents; and if they drink any deadly thing, it shall not hurt them; they shall lay hands on the sick, and they shall recover.'** So then after the Lord had spoken unto them; he was received up into heaven, and sat on the right hand of God."

In a world where a lot of humanitarianism and social works have been done by the church, there is a need to define what a mission trip based on the great commission really looks like. In response to that question, we wrote our own statement. By it, we train, equip, and send the saints out!

The Kingdom of God is not a matter of eating and drinking. But peace and joy in the Holy Ghost (**Romans 14:17**). For the Kingdom of God is not a matter of words. But power (**1 Corinthians 4:20**). The Kingdom of God is not a matter of making people happy. But bringing them to brokenness. The Kingdom of God is not a matter of building hospitals. But healing the sick. The Kingdom of God is not a matter of having pity on people. But of cleaning them of every disease. The Kingdom of God is not a matter of giving out glasses. But of recovering the sight of the blind. The Kingdom of God is not a matter of psychology. But of delivering the messed up mind. The Kingdom of God is not a matter of social works. But of speaking every word that proceeds out of the mouth of God. The Kingdom of God is not a matter of increasing the numbers of members. But of translating people into His marvelous light. The Kingdom of God is not a matter of making people accept Jesus. But of encouraging them to pick up the cross. The Kingdom of God is not a matter of giving license to sin. But of producing fruits of repentance.

The Kingdom of God is not a matter of being Christian. But of being born again, baptized in the Holy Spirit and in fire! The Kingdom of God is a matter of rooting out, pulling down, tearing up, throwing down but also building and planting incorruptible seeds by the hands of those that God has set over the nations and over any other kingdom:

That is the Apostolic Church and an Apostolic mission trip is the fruit thereof. So as you go, proclaim the message: **"And saying, Repent ye: for the kingdom of heaven is at hand." Matthews 3:2**

6) FIRE & INTIMACY WITH HIM: THE BEST TRAINING!

"For our God is all consuming fire, a jealous God." Deuteronomy 4:24

The fire of God comes to consume you and burn away the chaff of the World. You will be a house of fire. God is going to blaze this place. I believe it. We need His fire. He desires us to be purified by this fire — to be a flame for God with His fire burning in our hearts, in our minds, and in our bones. Do you burn for Him? Are you hot or cold or just lukewarm? God says you better be hot — a flame of love burning as a burnt sacrifice for our God. We need to stay on the altar, spend time at His feet. Be a burning log for God, and people around you will want what you have!

God will test you and refine you **(Psalm 66:10-15)**. We need not only the baptism with water unto repentance, but we need the **BAPTISM WITH THE HOLY SPIRIT AND WITH FIRE! (Matthew 3:11-12)**. He came to send fire on the earth. Are you ready? You are called to be a flame of fire **(Hebrews 1:7)**. With this fire in your belly, you will set your neighbor on fire for Him, and your community will be different, transformed! Be a living sacrifice, holy, acceptable to God (**Romans 12:1-2 / 1 John 1:5-6**). Be H.O.T.--- A House of Truth for Him!

"**And unto the angel of the church of the Laodiceans write; These things saith the Amen, the faithful and true witness, the beginning of the creation of God; I know thy works, that thou art neither cold nor hot: I would thou wert cold or hot. So then because thou art lukewarm, and neither cold nor hot, I will spew thee out of my mouth." Revelation 3:14-16**

For so long we have seen people being appointed by man, but we encourage you to be led by the Spirit of God! Not by might, not by power, not by denomination, but by the Spirit of the living God!

THE HOLY SPIRIT IS THE ONE WHO COMPELS YOU. NOT COLD. NOT LUKEWARM. BE H.O.T. FOR HIM

There is no better school than the school of the Holy Spirit. He will teach you all things!

THE HOLY SPIRIT IS THE ONE THAT TRAINS YOU, APPOINTS YOU, AND EMPOWERS YOU!

Seek Him and be ready to get the fire that never goes out!

The Five Giants of the Land (apostles, prophets, evangelists, teachers and pastors) together with the whole body of Christ — each member in his right position is marching on, taking the land, setting the captives free, bringing justice to the poor, practicing the pure religion: **"Pure religion and undefiled religion before God and the Father is this: to visit the fatherless and widows in their affliction, and to keep himself unspotted from the world" (James 1:27),** is to proclaim the pure gospel of Jesus Christ without any other motivation than to make the name of Jesus Christ known to every soul. The world will not resist the wisdom and the spirit by which you speak according to **Acts 6:10.** Do you want to see thousands of people repenting at Jesus' feet after one simple message? Let us go to the upper room because the Lord is ready to **"pour out His Spirit upon all flesh: and your sons and your daughters shall prophesy, and your young men shall see visions, and your old men shall dream dreams. And on my servants and on my handmaidens I will pour out in those days of my Spirit and they shall prophesy. I will show wonders in heaven above, and signs in the earth..." Acts 2: 17-19**

"YOU WILL receive POWER when the Holy Ghost comes upon you, and you will be HIS witnesses in your community, in your surrounding areas, in your country, and to the uttermost parts of the earth." Acts 1:8

Be baptized in the Holy Spirit and in Fire! Let's be **H.O.T.**

"I know thy works, that thou art neither cold nor hot: I would thou wert cold or hot. So then because thou art lukewarm, and

neither cold nor hot, I will spue thee out of my mouth."
Revelation 3:15-17

He paid the price with His own life so that **we are HIS
CHURCH, HIS BRIDE!** Hallelujah! The Spirit and the Bride
say, **"Come, Lord Jesus, come!"** First love is back! We are
passionate for Him and for souls, and we are fully equipped to
take the land and to bring salvation to all men! In the name of
Jesus Christ!

Decree and declare: Say this (I'M READY)

I'm a follower of Jesus Christ.

I'm a true disciple.

God help me not to be deceived.

God help me to be on fire for you.

Show me the new way.

Make me single minded.

Change my thinking.

Give me true peace and joy.

Remove all fear from me.

Make me bold.

Seal my heart, my mind, and my soul.

Let me drink from your cup the real new wine.

Circumcise my heart.

Make me totally devoted to you.

Give me enough love for you so I will pay the cost whatever it takes.

I will keep my vow and I will follow you.

I will not deny you and your Word. I will obey.

Not by might, not by power, but by your Holy Spirit

and by my passion for you, Jesus.

You are worthy of all!

In Jesus name I speak it and prophesy it over me!

7
AWAKENING THE GIANTS

"Father, we thank you for your Word, for your Truth. Thank you for leading us into all Truth. Father, we want to do "church" with power. Power from on high! We thank you for the spirit of wisdom, of revelation, and of the knowledge of you. Give us understanding of the deep things of you. Let us know your heart for this nation and for the nations of the Earth. I ask you, Lord, to hide me behind the cross so everything that comes out of my mouth will be from you!"

An apostolic church is rising up in the land. An apostolic church is what God desires. He is doing a new thing, and now it will spring forth. It is time to empty ourselves of old thinking and old traditions. Jesus appeared to Paul and ordained Him to preach the Gospel.

Our traditions make the Gospel of no effect. The church is not here only to cater to people but to obey the voice of

God. In obeying the voice of God, people will be catered to, but the way that God wants. We have a false love movement in the USA. They say, "Love people until they come to the Truth," but when you do that, because you want the church to be full of people, you start allowing spirits to come into the church, and those spirits begin to take over. Because this person wants to do something this way and the devil will send somebody else with a lot of money that wants to do something that way, and all of a sudden, the church is being done the way that people want to do it, but God has a blueprint from heaven! He has His own plan and the church that He is raising up is the church where the gates of hell will not prevail and where the glory of God rests — a resting place for Him. Not a lukewarm hub.

We have churches all over the place, but God is not there. Because if the church is not casting out demons, healing the sick, and preaching the Gospel with power, then that church is not really authentic from heaven's perspective. It has been man-ipulated. Because everywhere that Jesus went, that is what He did. Everywhere that Paul went, that's what He did. Even a deacon like Stephen did. The problem is not the generation. It is bad leadership full of compromising.

I am speaking to leaders right now. If you give heed to what I am saying, God will give you everything you need to build His church in your nation, not built by the hands of man but by the Holy Spirit. God has apostles, prophets, teachers, evangelists and pastors to equip and raise them up. Get your hands out of the way. Stop Babylonian man-pleasing,

Hollywood Christianity that only promotes presence without change. Presence without fire is a church without change.

God wants everyone to depend on Him, not on man. Our job as leaders in the church is to wean people off the dependency of man and to show them their identity so they can depend on Jesus. Because when we make people depend on us, it is really wrong because we, as leaders, are not made to handle the weight of it. It is the pride of Pharisees. People will start asking you to carry their burdens. All of this is being put on the leaders, and they end up not having time to spend in His presence, so let them go to God with their needs. We are not God, He is in us. We are gifts to be given. We give our lives, but we are not God!

We begin to lose His glory when people start looking at us. Jesus talked about those who love having their name called out in the market place, "Pastor, Pastor;" those that love to look different, to dress different. They love titles. Their chairs are bigger; they are on the pedestal. In the religion system, people carry the apostle and the prophet around on their high chair. They love to be served, but God is looking for the others to pour out the new wine, to give their lives like Paul and Jesus, those that have the attitude to serve one another. Jesus said to become the greatest in the Kingdom is to become the servant of all. Jesus said, "I came to give my life for ransom. I did not come to be served but to serve." And "to serve" means to minister!

So, the fivefold ministers - apostle, prophet, evangelist, pastor and teacher - should be ministering unto the Lord more than anybody else, and the Lord ministering to them. Then they come with what the Lord gave to them, and they minister to the people. Then the people should be ministering unto the Lord as well. In that ministering to one another, there is no division, no favoritism. To the ones with a little or big power, little or much anointing, let honor always be given! What God wants is not what man figures out in the fleshy mind. How to grow their church? Yes, that's the problem: It is their church. It doesn't matter what they say. If they don't do what Abba Daddy says, then they are an institute and a carnal church.

Don't let the false teachers and false grace preaching tell you that the blood of Jesus will keep covering you, so keep on sinning. No! The blood of Jesus will give you power to overcome it!

Anyone in Christ, leader or not, is marked for greatness! Imagine you and everyone in the Body becoming a legend to the World. Imagine people saying this tomorrow about today: "What was birthed in here transformed this nation," all the spiritual borders being opened and all the false religion being pushed out of this land. The Truth of the Word of God was exposed because the power of the Gospel of Jesus Christ was not in word only, not in tradition, but it was in the power of transformation. Jesus came to give us life and life more abundantly. He did not say only this nation, that nation, and that nation. He said EVERY NATION that makes this God their God, and every nation that receives a prophet receives a prophet's reward!

Daniel in the midst of Babylon brought transformation to that nation, but he also brought persecution because they did not bow down to the other god of Nebuchadnezzar. Many others have not bowed down to Baal. God said, "I still have seven thousand." Many leaders are bowing down to the Gospel of Prosperity, to the riches of this world. I am talking to leaders that will be shepherds over many sheep! Don't lord over them, but raise them up into sons and daughters of the living God, into the full stature of Christ, and if you have held back any truth from anybody, that means you love yourself more than them! Because love will cost you everything! Love without truth is not love; it is selfishness. Tickling ears will make you popular, but the remnant cannot be tickled. If your ears want be itched, you don't want this cross.

So many leaders have said, "Oh, this is too heavy for them." If it is in the Word of God, it is ready for anybody! God will feed them by His Spirit. Paul did not change the Word of God. He changed his approach, but he never changed the Word. Paul came with understanding. He knew where people were coming from but did not change the weight of the Word. He changed the approach of the Word. That is a big difference. We must understand where people are coming from but bring the same cross, the same Gospel, with the understanding. That is called Spirit led ministry – not tickling ear ministry. Paul never took out or added in. So many are doing that because they want a big church. Your foundation is the most important thing. Your foundation has to be the Word of God! If it is not upon the rock, the bigger you grow, the harder you will fall!

Today, I am coming to you to ensure your foundation, to make sure that it is upon the Word of God. Build on the rock! There is no other way! That is the problem with religion and tradition or building anything upon man's opinion! The Gospel that you preach must be founded on the Word of God! If it is in the Word of God, you have to believe it, you have to preach it, you cannot water it down, because if you do then you have lost the fear of the Lord! You are becoming god.

We need to live by the Word of God, not by the opinion of man or the ways of man, but by the Word of God! Who will be the one that will hear, "Good and faithful servant?" Not good and faithful apostle, not prophet, not evangelist, not teacher! On that day we all become one! Don't think you will get a reward as a leader just because you are doing what God told you to do! If you are living for rewards today, you are living for the wrong reasons! Don't expect any favor from God, because favor comes through obedience. You can be doing all the right things with a wrong heart and not have favor. God is changing our hearts. The Word is changing our minds.

The Holy Spirit is changing the church. We are either in or out of the will of God. There are no different types of churches. There is ONE. One Spirit. One bride. One Gospel. There are many other doctrines out there, but only one carries the power of God. God demands a church without the influence of the Spirit of Jezebel, Balaam, and the works of Nicolaitans. Chose today to be that one!

Father, I want to do "church," your church. If there is anything that is blocking us from seeing your glory, strip it away. Even if we need deliverance from anger, depression, unforgiveness, heal us so we can heal others. Today will be my day! Some things are torn in the flesh; some things are just flesh. Father, I pray that the sleeping giant will be awakened as we pray. Dreams and visions, hope inside of us, let it be activated. Let today be the day of new awakening, new authority, sound mind, clear vision. Father, give us vision. Paul said, **"O king of Agrippa, I will obey the heavenly vision."**

Let us hold Your heavenly vision! Apostolic vision is the heavenly vision! Let this be your vision. We will raise up a church that the gates of hell will not prevail, we will equip the saints, we will impart the gifts, we will raise disciples, we will encourage people to go through the fire because we will not partner with devils. We will be the book of Acts! You promise the latter rain shall be greater. We will be rain carriers! We don't need a name. We just need the Holy Spirit, seeing one another by the Holy Spirit. Father, we pray for a strong foundation on the apostles and prophets with Jesus being the first, as the cornerstone. It all started with Jesus, the alpha and the omega, the first and the last. He is the first Word, and He will be the last Word. He was the first love. He will be the last love. This is the only church that we can be part of.

Crucify the old man today! Pick up your cross! Father, we seal this word. We bless this nation. We bless these leaders, your servants! I want to hear reports that revival broke out all over this nation because of the seed of Truth. It never stops! The Word will run all over your country, not by advertisement, but by the power of God.

Let the oil run down to the whole body. No old wine will be poured out unto the sons of righteousness. The old is not good enough! Jesus said, "I am not a God of the dead but of the living." Those who want to drink and eat His flesh and blood will. Let the dead bury the dead. Let the crowd worship the crowd. Pick up the cross and follow Me, and I will show you things you have never seen before. I will move among you because I have torn the veil! Walk in your identity! See what you have: the kingdom of God inside of you! It is here! Let us walk in it. "The same power that raised Me up," Jesus said, "is in you! You need to lose yourself to find your place in Me. Not because of you but because of Me. I have ordained you to be in the fivefold ministry, not to make your name great, but to make My name great! Lose yourself, and yes, they will know you because they will know the God inside of you!"

8
HEAVENLY VISION

CAN YOU SEE IT NOW?

" I will stand upon my watch, and set me upon the tower, and will watch to see what he will say unto me, and what I shall answer when I am reproved. And the LORD answered me, and said, Write the vision, and make it plain upon tables, that he may run that readeth it. For the vision is yet for an appointed time, but at the end it shall speak, and not lie: though it tarry, wait for it; because it will surely come, it will not tarry. Behold, his soul which is lifted up is not upright in him: but the just shall live by his faith." Habakkuk 2:1-4

"Write the vision. Write the vision. Write the vision. When God speaks, write the vision and make it plain if you carry a mandate from God. It will surely come to pass. Wait and it will speak and loudly. It will be.

You can have a vision. There are two kinds of visions: one spiritual and one prophecy; both can come in the same way! So, we all serve God. We are not serving man, but we are stewarding a vision. So, it is God that we are serving. He is just putting pieces together. He is fitly joining every part to do His will on Earth.

All these had a mandate: Moses, Noah, Paul, Jesus, Peter, Joshua, Gideon, David, and so many more, and they all had God working with them!!! Blueprints from heaven, carrying specific instructions from God! We all are instructed in the Word by God concerning our character, but He instructs the living, alive in Christ now, concerning purposes ordained from heaven. Religion is dead so everyone gets instruction from a dead letter, and the end always will be dead works, but God has an end time purpose, and it is apostolic. Those who follow that vision will be endued with power to accomplish it.

John had a vision and released it to the Body. The book of Revelation is full of it. We are tarrying for that now, but God also gave Paul his own personal will and instruction, and up to this day, many are following it.

We submit to the vision, but if it is not of God, you better run from it. Brick upon brick: that is God establishing a vision. When the blueprint does not come from heaven, the vision surely does not come from Him. Nehemiah was restoring the gates, and God is using the apostolic to restore the end time bride - the Church. The biggest enemy of God's plans and purpose is religion.

"But rise, and stand upon thy feet: for I have appeared unto thee for this purpose, to make thee a minister and a witness both of these things which thou hast seen, and of those things in the which I will appear unto thee; Delivering thee from the people, and from the Gentiles, unto whom now I send thee, To open their eyes, and to turn them from darkness to light, and from the power of Satan unto God, that they may receive forgiveness of sins, and inheritance among them which are sanctified by faith that is in me. Whereupon, O king Agrippa, I was not disobedient unto the heavenly vision: But shewed first unto them of Damascus, and at Jerusalem, and throughout all the coasts of Judaea, and then to the Gentiles, that they should repent and turn to God, and do works meet for repentance."
Acts 26:16-20

Paul had a mandate. He had to do it exactly how God told him to. Whatever He told him to do, he did it, not more, not less. When we decide to do it God's way, there is no division among us. God is gathering. What is the vision for the bride down here: to destroy the works of darkness, to walk in the full measure of Christ. He gave this mandate to the apostles to lay foundations and start the church. Now He is giving the end time church vision to the apostles of today for the end times. There is an Ishmael apostolic network, but it is not from God. They are so engaged in the world, and it is counterfeit because they do not have the Spirit of Elijah. It's all mixture. Pray God will show you.

When we are together, we are protecting the heavenly vision. Be faithful to what God put in front of you! Serve that! We serve God, and He has His mandate for us. Organized religion has a form of God but lacks the anointing and the power!

"Wherefore comfort yourselves together, and edify one another, even as also ye do. And we beseech you, brethren, to know them which labour among you, and are over you in the Lord, and admonish you; And to esteem them very highly in love for their work's sake. And be at peace among yourselves. Now we exhort you, brethren, warn them that are unruly, comfort the feebleminded, support the weak, be patient toward all men. See that none render evil for evil unto any man; but ever follow that which is good, both among yourselves, and to all men. Rejoice evermore. Pray without ceasing. In every thing give thanks: for this is the will of God in Christ Jesus concerning you. Quench not the Spirit. Despise not prophesyings. Prove all things; hold fast that which is good. Abstain from all appearance of evil. And the very God of peace sanctify you wholly; and I pray God your whole spirit and soul and body be preserved blameless unto the coming of our Lord Jesus Christ. Faithful is he that calleth you, who also will do it." 1 Thessalonians 5:11-24

We are in Christ. We are seated with Him in heavenly places. God is making us ready for persecution, betrayal, attacks, but keep following the heavenly vision. If you don't have a heavenly vision, what are you going to do? Everything will vanish away. Only the eternal purposes will be left. Everything else will burn away. The Bible says to know those who labor among you. Why? Because they are either part of the vision or they are in division.

The Bible never said, "Be nice but preach the Truth." People that really want Jesus will look through your flesh, and they will see your passion and will give attention to what you are saying because it comes from a real place.

Man cannot promote you. If God has not promoted you, you have gone nowhere. Stick to the heavenly vision. Get with a vision and that heavenly vision will keep you. God will sustain you.

Itching ears' messages will fill a building, but the building is missing the One. God is not even there. But God has a vision. He set the apostles first in the church because they carry the vision. King Agrippa, whatever you said to me it won't matter. I will be faithful to the vision given by God to me. It doesn't matter about Pharaoh or Caesar. It is about the King of the World. "Nebuchadnezzar, I bow only to one master..."

Winds of doctrines are blowing all over the internet. It is attacking heavenly vision. A term I hate that the spirit of religion uses is, "We all have different tastes. Not everyone likes chocolate, pick your flavor." Give me a break. God is fitly joining us together. He is the master builder. If He does not build the house, we labor in vain. He has One Spirit, One doctrine, One church, and ONE FLAVOR. Religion always cuts up the Body and gives people what they want. Denomination comes from this apostate thinking. Then the devil will say, "Can we just agree to disagree?" NO. I only agree with God. What if Noah's sons would have said, "Father Noah, this is a better and faster way?" Would the boat float in times of rain? Noah got the blueprints and the vision, and His entire family obeyed it, and all were saved. Stick to the vision.

Make sure you do whatever God tells you with zeal. We don't hold back the truth because we have all the light the World needs. Or all you will be doing is self-help. That has nothing to do with the cross and its power and for the Truth. Religion is backwards because they want to control. They take from God becoming Jezebel instead of the sons of Noah.

Mandate is about a vision. The Spirit will tell you directly who, what, and how. This is not our home, so we need a heavenly vision for down here. Stephen was a deacon, anointed, but he came under apostolic vision and got killed because of it, but he did it. Because He came to serve the vision he moved in the same power as the vision stewards.

We need to understand the difference between organized religion and purpose. Now to move and to manifest His kingdom will be only those under the heavenly vision. The vision cannot be accomplished in the flesh. Rejoice that we are one with Christ. So, we have only one vision: HIS!

If you don't have a vision, don't make yourself a prostitute with a gift. Connect with a vision because that is why you have that gift. Then you will see the anointing like never before. Your gift connected to a heavenly vision will birth destiny. Your gift on your own will birth a life of striving. Be free and see. Get on His vision. You may lose the vision if you don't have your eyes on Him. Keep on watching. Keep on praying. If you have the mind of Christ, you must think like Christ. What is your mandate? What is your vision?

It better be heavenly, apostolic, and if it is, surely it shall come to pass, but first you have to see it.

In Him,
Shane W Roessiger
H.O.T. House of Truth

TRUTH NOT FOR SALE

Freely we receive. Freely we give.

Free Books Available

www.hothouseoftruth.com

"Till we all come in the unity of the faith, and of the knowledge of the Son of God, unto a perfect man, unto the measure of the stature of the fullness of Christ." Ephesians 4

H.O.T. House of Truth – Apostolic Center
360 S Tamiami Trail – Nokomis – FL – (941) 412-5414
Equipping the Saints – Sending them out

Made in USA - Crawfordsville, IN
87800_9781720776932
02.12.2021 1759